RENAISSANCE MEDICINE

Nicola Barber

Chicago, Illinois

www.capstonepub.com
Visit our website to find out more information about Heinemann-Raintree books.

To order:
 Phone 800-747-4992
Visit www.capstonepub.com to browse our catalog and order online.

Edited by Andrew Farrow, Adam Miller, and
  Vaarunika Dharmapala
Designed by Philippa Jenkins
Picture research by Ruth Blair
Originated by Capstone Global Library Ltd
Printed and bound in China by Leo Paper
  Products Ltd

16 15 14 13 12
10 9 8 7 6 5 4 3 2 1

Library of Congress Cataloging-in-Publication Data
Barber, Nicola.
  Renaissance medicine / Nicola Barber.
    p. cm. — (Medicine through the ages)
  Includes bibliographical references and index.
  ISBN 978-1-4109-4644-7 (hb (freestyle)) — ISBN 978-1-4109-4650-8 (pb (freestyle)) 1. Medicine, Medieval. 2. Renaissance. I. Title.
  R141.B37 2013
  610.94 — dc23   2011031907

Acknowledgments
We would like to thank the following for permission to reproduce photographs: Corbis pp. 7, 10, 41 (© Bettmann), 19 (© Tetra Images), 31, 36 (© Stapleton Collection); Getty Images pp. 8, 23 (Hulton Archive), 27 (De Agostini), 33 (Hulton Archive/Universal History Archive); Science Photo Library pp. 5, 26 (NYPL/Science Source), 13 (CCI Archives); Wellcome Library, London pp. 4, 9, 11, 12, 15 (top), 15 (bottom), 16, 18, 20, 21, 22, 24, 25, 28, 29, 30, 32, 34, 35, 37, 38, 39, 40.

Cover photograph of an oil painting showing the interior of a surgeon's office, painted by a follower of David Teniers the Younger, reproduced with permission of Wellcome Library, London.

Every effort has been made to contact copyright holders of any material reproduced in this book. Any omissions will be rectified in subsequent printings if notice is given to the publisher.

Contents

Some words are shown in bold, **like this**. You can find out what they mean by looking in the glossary. You can also look out for them in the "Word Station" box at the bottom of each page.

New Ways of Thinking

The Renaissance was a period in European history that covered roughly the years 1400 to 1700. We have come to describe this period as the Renaissance, which means "rebirth," because it was a time of renewed interest in scholarship and learning in Europe. Such interest grew out of the increased wealth of the late Middle Ages, which in turn saw the founding of many universities in European cities.

In medicine, university-educated doctors learned from texts originally written by ancient Greek **physicians** such as Hippocrates, Dioscorides, and Galen. Many of these texts had been preserved in the Islamic world and then translated into Arabic before finding their way to Europe, where they were studied in Latin translations.

The woman in this painting is having her foot bled by a physician. **Bloodletting** (see page 29) was a common treatment throughout the Renaissance period.

Observation and experiment

European scholars of the Renaissance turned once again to the writings of Greek and Roman thinkers, often going back to the original texts and making their own translations and observations. In some cases, ideas that had been accepted for many centuries were challenged, such as Galen's ideas about **anatomy** (see pages 8–9).

This new spirit of questioning went hand-in-hand with an interest in observation and experimentation, which led to breakthroughs in the fields of anatomy and surgery. The Renaissance saw the birth of the scientific method, which involved conducting an experiment, writing down observations, and reaching a conclusion.

This book will examine the discoveries of physicians such as Andreas Vesalius (see pages 8–9) and William Harvey (see pages 14–17) that were major landmarks in medical history. Yet these discoveries had little or no immediate impact on the everyday lives of ordinary people. Medical beliefs and treatments changed very little for the majority of people in Renaissance Europe and the wider world.

The four humors

The theory of the four **humors** originated in the writings of the Greek physician Hippocrates (460 BCE TO C. 375 BCE). It was believed that the body contained four humors—phlegm, blood, yellow bile, and black bile. In a healthy person, these were in balance, while illness was caused by too much or too little of one of them. There were also personality types associated with each humor. This image shows a sanguine (optimistic) character at the top left, phlegmatic (unemotional) at the top right, choleric (irritable) at the bottom left, and melancholic (sad) at the bottom right. The aim of treatments was to bring the humors back into balance.

humor in medieval and Renaissance medical theory, one of the four important fluids that control the body

New theories and inventions

In 1543, a Polish scientist named Nicolaus Copernicus published his theory that Earth orbited the Sun. Early in the 17th century, Copernicus's theory was supported by Italian scientist Galileo Galilei, based on observations made through an exciting new invention — the telescope. Galileo was put under house arrest by the Catholic Church. The theory went against one of the Church's basic teachings — that Earth is the center of the universe. Church leaders feared that people would start questioning Church teachings on other matters, too.

However, these new ideas spread rapidly around Europe, thanks to another groundbreaking invention — printing. In the 1430s, a German craftsman named Johannes Gutenberg developed a printing press that could print multiple copies of a book or pamphlet. Before this, copies of texts were made by hand, usually by religious men called monks. This work was difficult and slow, and texts were therefore treasured and often locked away in monastery libraries. New ideas could now reach many more people than before. The works of the Greek physician Galen were some of the earliest medical books to be printed.

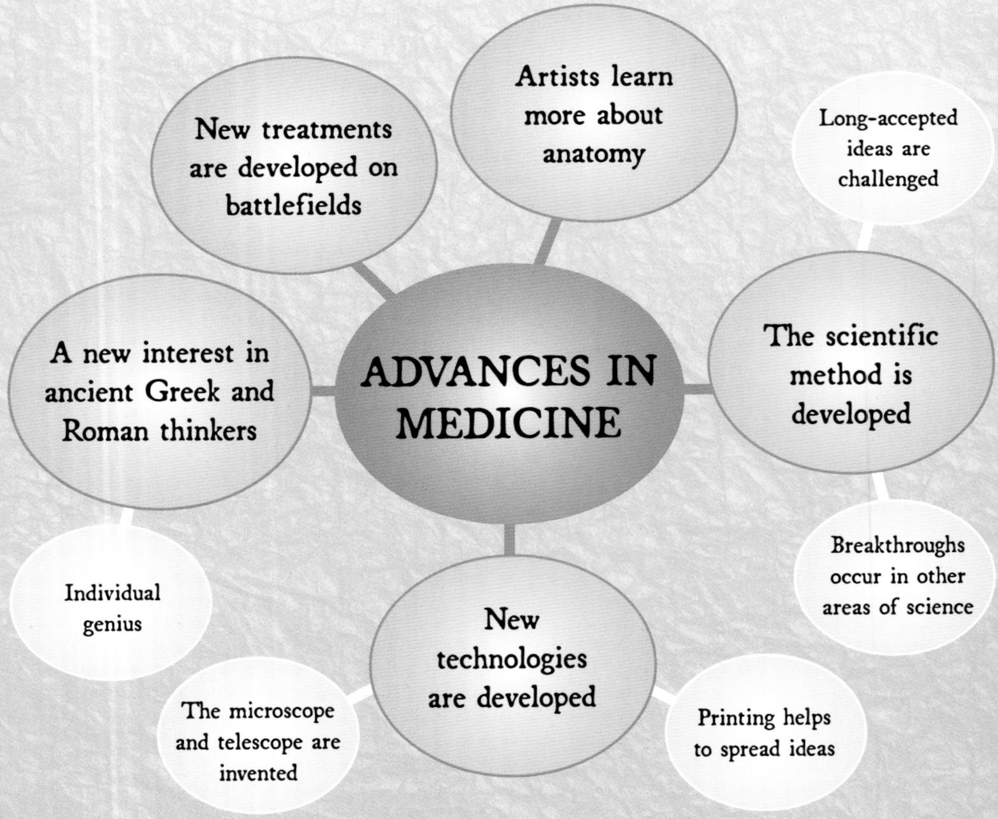

This diagram shows the factors that led to medical advances during the Renaissance.

New treatments are developed on battlefields

Artists learn more about anatomy

Long-accepted ideas are challenged

A new interest in ancient Greek and Roman thinkers

ADVANCES IN MEDICINE

The scientific method is developed

Individual genius

New technologies are developed

Breakthroughs occur in other areas of science

The microscope and telescope are invented

Printing helps to spread ideas

The Italian artist Leonardo da Vinci observed several dissections and made detailed anatomical studies of the human body.

THE MICROSCOPE

Although the idea of using a lens to magnify objects had long been known, the first workable compound microscope (using more than one lens) was made in the Netherlands in the 1590s by two eyeglass-makers—Zacharias Janssen and his father, Hans. The microscope was further developed in the 1600s by another Dutchman, Anton van Leeuwenhoek.

Anatomical drawing

Dissections of the human body had been forbidden by the Catholic Church for much of the medieval period. In the 14th century, however, dissections began to take place in Italy. Many medical textbooks printed from the mid-16th century onward—for example, the works of Vesalius (see pages 8–9)—were illustrated with detailed anatomical drawings.

Breakthroughs in Surgery

In 1543, a Flemish **physician** named Andreas Vesalius published *De humani corporis fabrica* ("The Structure of the Human Body"). This work was based on Vesalius's own **dissections** of human bodies. His observations led him to challenge many of the ideas of the Greek physician Galen.

Dissection

In the 2nd century CE, Galen **dissected** animals to improve his surgical skills and to learn about **anatomy**. Under Roman law, he was not permitted to work on human bodies, so he based his understanding of human anatomy on animals such as pigs and goats. Galen made many insightful observations based on these dissections, but his understanding of human anatomy was clearly limited. From the 14th century, some dissections of the corpses of executed criminals began in Italy, in order to teach students at the new medical schools that were being established there. The Church accepted this.

This painting shows medical students observing a dissection at a hospital in Delft, the Netherlands, in 1617.

The dissections that Vesalius attended as a student at the University of Paris, France, in the 1530s were typical of the time. The work of cutting up the body was carried out by assistants, while the physician read aloud from the works of Galen. The assistants did the cutting because surgery was considered to be of low status. In 1537, Vesalius became professor of surgery and anatomy at the University of Padua, in Italy. He decided the only way to learn more about human anatomy was to perform dissections himself—a radical idea at that time.

Challenging old ideas

Vesalius began to realize that what he was observing in his own dissections did not always match what was described in Galen's work. He published his findings in *De humani corporis fabrica* and worked with several artists to produce accurate anatomical illustrations.

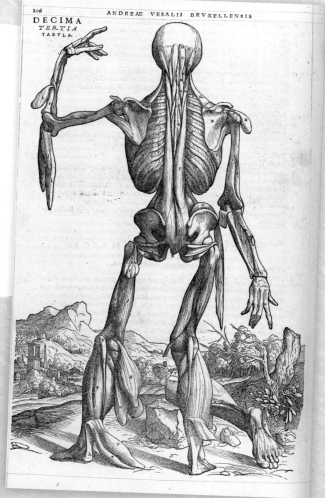

This page from Book Seven of Vesalius's *De humani corporis fabrica* shows the human skeleton from the back.

▶

COMMON CONFUSIONS

The jawbone

Galen's use of animals for dissection had resulted in confusion between animal and human anatomy. His dissections of dogs had led him to believe that the human jawbone was made up of two bones. Vesalius was able to show that the lower jaw in humans is only one bone. This was just one of about 200 corrections to Galen's theories that Vesalius made.

Surgical discoveries

In 1536, a surgeon named Ambroise Paré joined the French army. His first experience of battle, and of dealing with gunshot wounds, was in the same year. At the time, the accepted way of dealing with wounds was to **cauterize** them by pouring on hot oil—a very painful procedure. While treating the injured soldiers, Paré ran out of oil. According to the account he later wrote in his *Method of Treating Wounds* (1545), Paré quickly mixed up an ointment of egg yolk, turpentine, and rose oil. He applied this ointment to the wounds and covered them with bandages.

When Paré checked on the soldiers the next day, he found to his amazement that the ones he had treated with ointment were in a much better condition than those whose wounds had been cauterized. The turpentine acted as an **antiseptic**, although Paré would not have understood this. He vowed never to use cauterization on gunshot wounds again.

AMBROISE PARÉ
(1510–1590)

Paré trained as a **barber-surgeon** (see pages 34–35) in Paris, before joining the army as a surgeon in 1536. His medical textbooks—*Method of Treating Wounds* (1545) and *Works* (1575)—were published in his native language French (rather than in Latin), which made them available to a much wider audience. He became royal surgeon in 1552 and served four French kings. The painting to the right shows Paré treating a wounded soldier.

Did you know?
Paré designed artificial limbs to replace limbs that were removed in amputations. An artificial leg pictured in Paré's *Works* featured a movable knee joint controlled by a string as well as a flexible foot operated by a spring.

WORD STATION
cauterize in medieval and Renaissance medicine, to "seal" wounds by applying boiling oil or hot irons

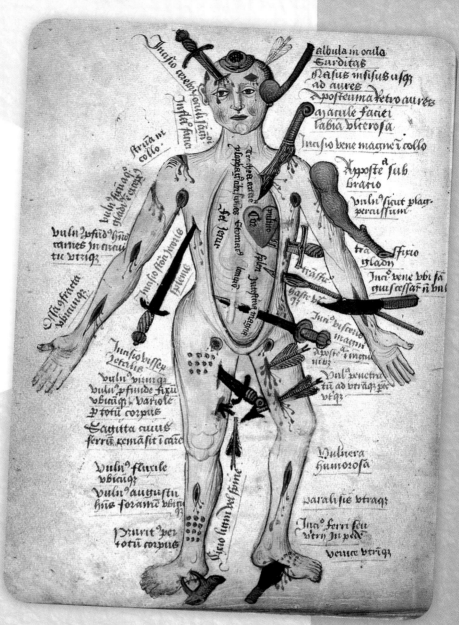

This is a "wound man" diagram from the mid-15th century. It shows the types of wounds a person might experience in battle. The surrounding text gives treatments for the different injuries.

Battlefield surgery

Like Paré, battlefield surgeons often found themselves working in difficult conditions. However, the need to come up with new solutions on the spot meant that surgeons learned quickly and often acquired new skills. The kinds of wounds being treated changed considerably from the 15th century onward, when gunpowder began to be used in battle. Instead of the relatively clean wounds inflicted by swords or pikes, surgeons were faced with torn flesh and shattered bones. Before Paré's breakthrough, they believed that the gunpowder poisoned the wounds and that the only way to prevent the poison from spreading was by cauterization.

Ligatures

Paré spent many more years working as an army surgeon. The causes of infection in wounds were not understood at that time, and often the only solution was to amputate (cut off) the affected limb. The greatest danger to the patient was loss of blood. To try to stop the bleeding, a red-hot iron, called a cautery, was applied to the stump. Once again, Paré came up with an alternative method. He tied silk threads, called **ligatures**, around each cut blood vessel to stop the bleeding. However, although this procedure worked, we now know that there was a high risk of introducing infection into the wound from the ligatures.

Richard Wiseman

The 17th-century English surgeon Richard Wiseman knew the work and methods of Paré well. Wiseman had served as a surgeon in the Dutch and Spanish navies, as well as on the battlefields on land. He became royal surgeon when England's King Charles II was restored to the throne in 1660. Wiseman wrote two books: *A Treatise on Wounds* (1672) and *Several Chirurgical [Surgical] Treatises* (1676).

Richard Wiseman worked as a surgeon in the king's army during the English Civil War (1642–1651).

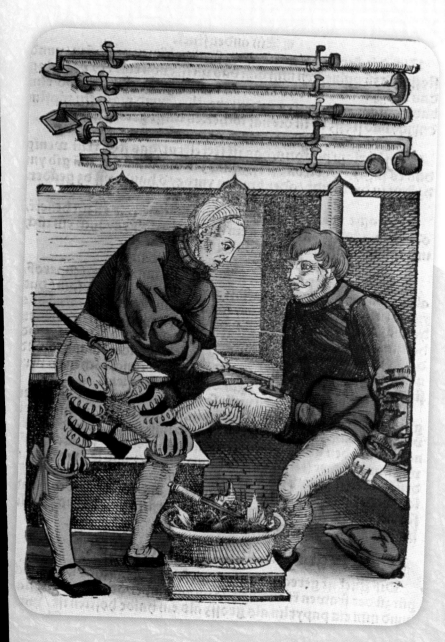

This 16th-century engraving shows a surgeon pressing a red-hot iron to his patient's wound in order to cauterize it. More irons are shown hanging on the wall.

MIRACLE CURE?

In his role as royal surgeon, Richard Wiseman attended ceremonies in which sick people came to the king of England for a cure. It was generally believed that the king had the power to heal illnesses by touch. These illnesses, known as the "king's evil," included scrofula, a skin disease caused by tuberculosis. Whether or not Wiseman genuinely believed that the king had healing powers, it would have been treason to deny it.

Although Wiseman used Paré's methods of tying ligatures to stop bleeding, his accounts of surgery in the heat of battle make it clear that often there was not time for such careful work. Amputations and cauterizing were still common and necessary procedures. He wrote: "In heat of Fight, whether it be at Sea or Land, the Chirurgeon [surgeon] ought to consider at the first Dressing, what possibility there is of preserving the wounded Member; and accordingly, if there be no hopes of saving it, to make his Amputation at that instant whilst the Patient is free of Fever…" (from *Several Chirurgical Treatises*).

Scientific Advances

One of the pioneers of a scientific approach to medical study was an English **physician** named William Harvey. Working in the early 17th century, Harvey used observation and experimentation to describe correctly for the first time how blood circulated around the body.

Before Harvey's work, most people still referred back to the ancient texts of Galen as the absolute authority on this subject. Galen's theory stated that blood was formed in the liver and then circulated in the **veins** before being burned up by the body. Although Galen's ideas had been challenged by a few physicians before Harvey, it was Harvey's publication in 1628 of *Concerning the Motion of the Heart and Blood* that set out a new theory of circulation.

Harvey's theory caused controversy among many people who were unwilling to question Galen. Despite this, it had become well established by the time of Harvey's death in 1657.

This diagram shows how ideas about the circulation of blood developed from Galen onward. You can see how knowledge is lost, rediscovered, and passed on.

Galen
(129–c. 216 CE)

He held the theory that blood passes from one side of the heart to the other through holes in the septum, in the middle of the heart. This was the widely accepted theory in Europe until the 17th century.

Ibn al-Nafis
(1213–1288)

An Arab physician, he disputed Galen's theory and described the circulation of blood between the lungs. However, his work remained unknown in Europe.

Marcello Malpighi
(1628–1694)

By studying blood through a microscope, Malpighi was able in 1661 to describe the **capillary** network, which backed up and completed Harvey's theory of blood circulation.

William Harvey
(1578–1657)

An English physician, he developed the work of Vesalius and Fabricius to prove that blood circulates around the body.

Hieronymus Fabricius
(1537–1691)

A professor at the University of Padua, Fabricius discovered **valves** in the veins that allow blood to go only one way. William Harvey was one of his students.

Andreas Vesalius
(1514–1564)

From his **dissections** of the human heart, Vesalius noted that blood could not travel through the septum.

Michael Servetus
(1511–1553)

This Spanish preacher described the movement of blood from the heart to the lungs. He was burned at the stake for his religious beliefs, and his medical theories did not become widely known.

Matteo Realdo Colombo
(c.1516–1559)

He succeeded Vesalius as professor of surgery at the University of Padua, in Italy. He correctly identified and described the movement of blood through the heart and the lungs.

Harvey's experiments

Harvey developed his ideas on the circulation of blood from an important clue provided by Hieronymus Fabricius, his teacher at the University of Padua, in Italy. Fabricius had identified a system of valves in the veins, but he had not been able to explain their exact function. After many experiments on animals, Harvey was able to demonstrate that these valves were one-way flaps that allowed blood to move from the organs to the heart, but not to flow the other way.

From his dissections, Harvey estimated the capacity of the human heart. He figured out roughly how much blood was pumped by each heartbeat, and after many more experiments he realized that the blood flowed in a circle around the body. Based on these observations, he was able to disprove Galen's theories that blood formed in the liver and that it was absorbed into the body.

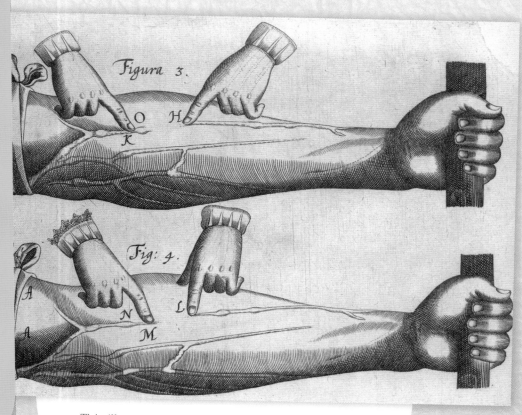

This illustration from William Harvey's *Concerning the Motion of the Heart and Blood* shows an experiment to demonstrate the working of valves in the veins.

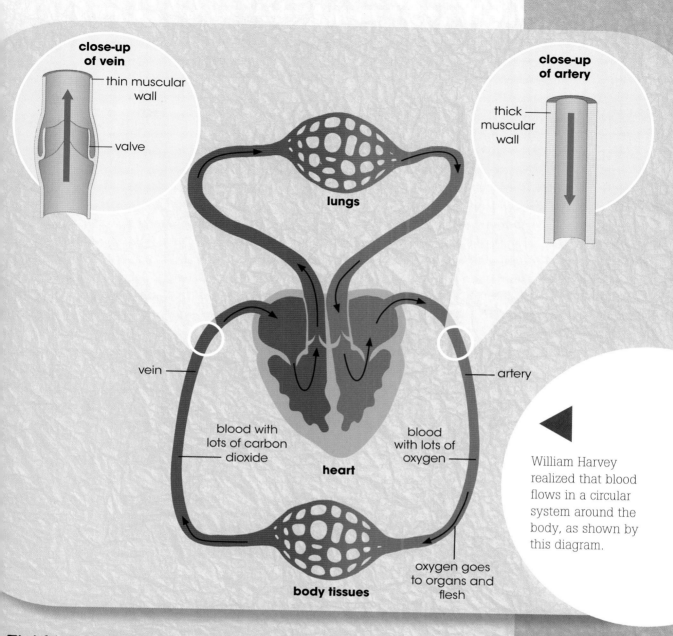

close-up of vein
— thin muscular wall
— valve

close-up of artery
thick muscular wall —

lungs

vein —

— artery

blood with lots of carbon dioxide —

blood with lots of oxygen —

heart

oxygen goes to organs and flesh

body tissues

William Harvey realized that blood flows in a circular system around the body, as shown by this diagram.

Finishing Harvey's work

Between the **arteries**, which deliver blood to the organs, and veins, which carry the blood back to the heart, lie tiny blood vessels called capillaries. Harvey correctly guessed the existence of the capillaries, but without a microscope he was unable to see them. This work was completed only a few years after his death by Marcello Malpighi, an Italian physician working at the University of Bologna, in Italy. In 1661, using a microscope, Malpighi identified and described the capillary network in the lungs of a frog.

The Royal Society had its origins in a group of natural philosophers (scientists) who met in London and Oxford, England, in the 1640s to acquire knowledge by "experimental investigation." The group included the chemist Robert Boyle, the architect and mathematician Christopher Wren, and Robert Hooke.

On November 28, 1660, members of the group decided to form "a Colledge for the Promoting of Physico-Mathematicall Experimentall Learning." This became The Royal Society of London for Improving Natural Knowledge. Its first **curator** of experiments was Robert Hooke.

Microscopic worlds

Malpighi continued his groundbreaking studies with the microscope in the 1660s and 1670s, observing and describing the taste buds, the **optic nerve**, and the layers of the skin. He also examined insects, such as the silkworm, and plants. His work attracted the attention of the Royal Society in London, England (see the box to the left), and in 1668 Malpighi began corresponding with members of the society. In 1669, Malpighi was made a member of the society, and from that time onward his findings were published by the Royal Society.

In Italy, however, Malpighi's work was the subject of controversy. Many people did not want to accept his findings because they went against the work of the ancient writers.

In England, a member of the Royal Society named Robert Hooke studied a wide range of materials under a microscope and published his findings in *Micrographia* ("Small Drawings") in 1665. The objects examined by Hooke included snowflakes, fossils, pieces of fabric, strands of hair, and shells.

This engraving of a flea is from Robert Hooke's *Micrographia*. The writer Samuel Pepys described it as "the most ingenious book that I ever read in my life."

This is a model of Anton van Leeuwenhoek's microscope. It had a screw for adjusting the height, a lens, and a piece to hold the object in place.

Hooke was the first person to use the word *cell* to describe the internal structure of a piece of cork. His work inspired a Dutch tradesman who was already experimenting with making different types of lenses. Anton van Leeuwenhoek devoted his life to microscopic research and he, too, reported his findings to the Royal Society.

Van Leeuwenhoek was the first to observe microscopic one-celled animals (protozoa) and **bacteria**, which he called "very little animalcules." He also gave the first accurate description of red blood cells. He was made a member of the Royal Society in 1680.

Renaissance Diseases

People in the Renaissance period experienced a wide range of illnesses and diseases, including **smallpox**, "sweating sickness" (probably influenza), and **dysentery** ("flux"). There was very little understanding of what caused these illnesses or how they were passed on. People continued to refer to the theory of the four **humors** (see page 5) to explain illness. The transmission of disease was widely thought to be caused by the presence of "bad air," or "miasma." It was believed that miasma carried invisible particles of rotting or decaying matter (leading to the bad smell) that entered the body.

There was little understanding of the link between hygiene and health. Towns and cities tended to be overcrowded and filthy, with narrow streets filled with garbage as well as animal and human waste. Such places were breeding grounds for disease-carrying pests such as rats, lice, and fleas. Disease affected wealthy and poor alike. In 1562, England's Queen Elizabeth I nearly died from smallpox. Lady Mary Sidney, who nursed the queen through her illness, then caught the disease herself. She was so badly scarred by the disease that she was forced to wear a mask whenever she appeared in public.

This medal was made to celebrate Queen Elizabeth I's recovery from smallpox with little scarring. It shows a hand shaking a snake into a fire, referring to an episode in the Bible in which St. Paul was bitten by a snake but was unharmed by its venom.

The plague

Over 200 years earlier, one of the most feared diseases had been the **plague**. The Black Death of 1347–1350 wiped out about one-third of the entire population of Europe. Outbreaks of the plague continued across Europe and the Islamic world throughout the Renaissance period. These outbreaks often centered on cities, where the disease was easily spread in the crowded and **unsanitary** conditions.

In the 15th century, plague doctors tried to protect themselves from "bad air" by wearing long robes, thick gloves, and a bird-like mask. The beak was stuffed with herbs, to keep away bad smells.

"DISEASE SEEDS"

In 1546, Girolamo Fracastoro, an Italian **physician**, suggested that disease was passed on by tiny particles or "seeds." He thought that infection was transferred from one person to the next by direct contact, on carriers such as clothes, or through the air. Fracastoro was also the originator of the name *syphilis* (see page 25), after writing a Latin poem about the disease.

The Great Plague

One of the last major outbreaks of the plague was the Great Plague of London in 1664–1666. The plague was terrifying and seemed to be unstoppable. It killed most of its victims very quickly, and it spread very rapidly.

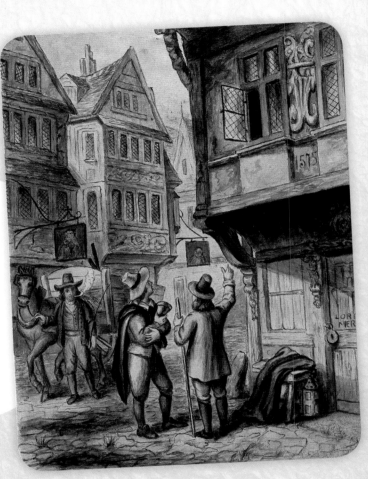

This painting from 1665 shows men arriving to cart away the dead from this house.

Since the Black Death, measures had been introduced in many European towns and cities to contain the spread of the plague. Some cities built large isolation hospitals—called pesthouses—where victims were sent at the first signs of disease.

Other cities, including London, had "plague orders" allowing local authorities to put families under house arrest if they were found to be infected. The house was marked with a red cross, and a guard was set to ensure no one entered or left. At night, "searchers" went into houses and took away dead bodies to be buried in mass pits.

Where did the plague come from?

Beliefs about the cause of the plague had changed little since the Black Death. Many people thought that the disease was God's punishment for human sins. Others looked at the movements of the stars and planets for an explanation. Today, many historians and scientists think that the plague was spread by rats. Others, however, argue that it was spread from person to person.

If rats were the real culprits, then one of the measures taken in 1665 to try to prevent the spread of plague—the slaughter of thousands of stray cats in London—would have had the opposite effect. It removed the main predators of the plague-infested rats.

This illustration was published in a newspaper in 1665. It shows the angel of death hovering over London during the Great Plague.

PEPYS AND THE PLAGUE

English government official Samuel Pepys (1633–1703) was a naval administrator who also famously kept a series of diaries in which he tracked the progress of the plague. Here he comes across several plague-struck houses and buys some tobacco to try to ward off "bad air":

"This day ... I did in Drury-lane see two or three houses marked with a red cross upon the doors, and 'Lord have mercy upon us' writ there—which was a sad sight to me ... I was forced to buy some roll tobacco to smell to and chaw [chew] ..."

Pepys was fortunate that he did not catch the plague.

MISERY

In *A Journal of the Plague Year* (1722), English writer Daniel Defoe described the desperation of those who were left behind: "But here again the misery of that time lay upon the poor who, being infected, had neither food or physic, neither physician or **apothecary** to assist them, or nurse to attend them. Many of those died calling for help, and even for sustenance [food and water], out at their windows in a most miserable and deplorable manner..."

How people were affected

The Great Plague started in late 1664 just outside London. During the summer months of 1665, the death rate soared, peaking in September, when 7,165 people died. We know the numbers of deaths thanks to records called Bills of Mortality that were compiled weekly after 1603. The total number of recorded deaths in the Great Plague was 68,596, but the true number was probably more than 100,000 by the end of the **epidemic** in 1666.

The Great Plague was also called the "Poore's Plague" because it affected poor people more than the wealthy. Anyone who could afford to travel left London.

However, the mayor and his councillors stayed to fight the plague. Some of the regulations issued by them show that links were being made between dirt and disease, even if they were not fully understood. For example, people were ordered to sweep the street outside their houses and to collect garbage for removal by "rakers."

This woodcut from 1630 shows wealthy people fleeing London during the Great Plague.

WORD STATION
apothecary person, mainly in the medieval and Renaissance periods, who prepared and dispensed medicines and remedies

Syphilis

Another disease that caused great fear during the Renaissance period was syphilis. This "new" disease was possibly brought into Europe from the Americas by sailors. It was often known as the "great pox," as one of its symptoms was sores and ulcers that looked similar to smallpox.

When it first arrived in Europe in the 1490s, it was a terrifying disease that killed many and often left survivors horribly disfigured. From the 1520s, it was known to be a sexually transmitted disease, and many people considered that sufferers should be punished rather than treated. In fact, it was most commonly treated with mercury, which we now know to be toxic (poisonous) to humans. Syphilis sufferers could often be recognized by their metallic-smelling breath and silvery-blue gums. These symptoms were the side-effects of taking mercury.

This woodcut of a man suffering from syphilis dates from 1496 and is believed to be by the German artist Albrecht Dürer. It is the earliest-known depiction of someone with syphilis. The date and the **astrological** chart at the top of the image may refer to a belief that syphilis was the result of planetary movements on the date shown.

THE MAYA AND THE INCA

South of Aztec lands was the empire of the Maya. Even further south, in the Andes Mountains, was that of the Inca. By 1526, the Spanish had reached Inca territory, and by the 1530s they had conquered them. As with the Aztecs, smallpox played a large part in their rapid defeat.

A new world

The voyages of Christopher Columbus to the Americas (1492–1504) opened up an entirely "New World" to Europeans. They came across small tribes of native Americans on the Caribbean islands where Columbus landed, but when the Spanish adventurer Hernan Cortés landed on the mainland in 1519, he came across the Aztec Empire. Cortés and his men were astonished by the Aztec capital, Tenochtitlán, which had drains and sewage systems, public **latrines**, and clean streets.

The Spanish brought with them diseases that had never been experienced in the Americas, including measles, smallpox, **typhoid**, and **scarlet fever**. This meant the people there had not built up immunity (natural protections) against any of these diseases.

Within months, hundreds of islanders in the Caribbean began to die, probably from influenza carried by pigs on Columbus's ships. Smallpox followed, and Cortés's men spread it to Tenochtitlán. When the Spanish attacked the city in 1521, its 300,000 inhabitants were already in the grip of a smallpox epidemic. Around half died. Thanks to smallpox, Cortés conquered the Aztecs with a force of only 300 men.

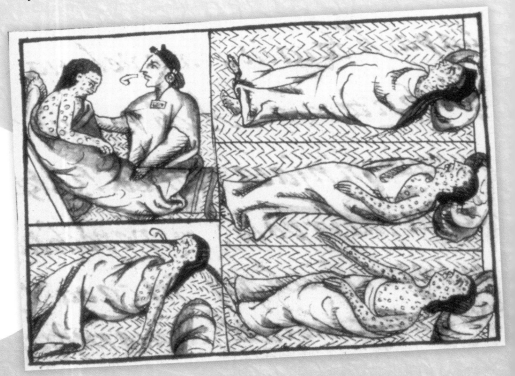

This illustration from a series of Spanish books compiled between 1540 and 1585 shows Aztecs dying from smallpox.

▶

A family tradition

The Spanish invaders were impressed by the knowledge of the Aztec medical profession. Some Aztec physicians specialized in religious ceremonies to the Aztec gods, who were believed to be responsible for specific illnesses. There were also surgeons, midwives, and bloodletters. Medical training was passed down within families, usually from a father to a son, although women were permitted to practice medicine, too. This illustration shows Aztec physicians preparing tobacco for use in healing.

The slave trade

The Europeans set up plantations and mines in South and Central America. They needed a workforce, but the death rate of the local populations was so high that they were forced to turn to a new source of labor. In 1518, the first Africans were brought on ships across the Atlantic Ocean to work as slaves. They brought with them more diseases that were previously unknown in the Americas, in particular malaria and yellow fever. There were many epidemics that wiped out hundreds of thousands of people.

Treatments

Most medical treatments in Renaissance Europe had changed little from medieval times. **Physicians** usually examined a patient's urine in order to **diagnose** an ailment. This diagnosis was based on the theory of the four **humors** (see page 5), so the aim of the treatment was to restore a healthy balance between the humors. Vomiting (throwing up) and **bloodletting** were the two most common ways to get rid of excess humors. Often a physician would check an **astrological** chart to decide on the best day of the month for treatment of a particular patient.

This painting shows a French apothecary's shop in the 1700s. Jars full of ingredients for remedies line the wall.

This is the title page from John Gerard's *Great Herball*. Much of the book was an English translation of an earlier herbal by a Dutch scholar named Rembert Dodoens, although Gerard added some plants from his own garden and from North America.

GREAT HERBALL

In 1597, John Gerard published his *Great Herball*, a catalog containing descriptions of over 1,000 plants. (An **herbal** is book that describes herbs and their uses.) The book contained the first picture ever seen in Europe of another introduction from the New World, the potato. It quickly became an extremely popular food.

Bloodletting

The simplest method of bloodletting was cutting into a **vein** with a scalpel and allowing the blood to flow into a bowl. Different veins were cut, usually by a **barber-surgeon** (see pages 34–35), depending on the health problem. Cupping was another common technique. A warmed cup was placed onto the skin to draw blood to the surface. Some physicians used leeches to draw off excess blood. These animals have tiny sharp teeth that bite through the skin. They then suck out blood until they are full.

Apothecaries

Physicians used medicines made from a wide variety of plants and other substances. These remedies were usually mixed up to order, sometimes by the physician, but often by an **apothecary**. The first apothecary shops had been set up in the Islamic world from the 8th century CE onward. In Renaissance Europe, apothecary shops were found in most towns. For people who could not afford to see a doctor, the apothecary's shop was often a useful place to go for advice, as well as for basic services such as teeth-pulling.

New World introductions

Voyagers to the New World brought large numbers of plants back to Europe. In 1571, a Spanish physician named Nicolas Monardes wrote a book about the medicinal plants of the New World, called in the English translation *Joyfull Newes out of the Newe Founde Worlde*. Some of the new plants were:

- *Guaiacum wood*: Gum from this wood was used to treat **syphilis**.

- *Ipecacuanha*: The root was used to make a syrup that caused vomiting.

- *Sarsaparilla and sassafras*: They were used in Europe to treat syphilis.

- *Vanilla*: This was used as a remedy for fever.

THE FIRST HERBAL IN THE AMERICAS

We know a great deal about Aztec remedies from a herbal written in 1552 by Martinus de la Cruz and Juannes Badianus. It illustrates and describes 204 medicinal herbs used by the Aztecs, as well as various treatments. It also lists minerals and crystals that were used in healing. For example, the emerald was used to treat a fractured head, in a lotion for **gout**, and in a potion for fever.

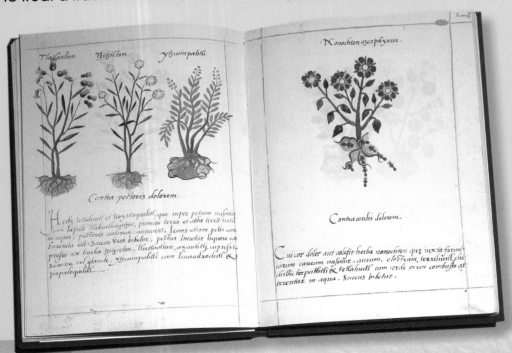

ALTERIVS NON SIT,QVI SVVS ESSE POTEST.

LAVS DEO, PAX VIVIS, REQVIES ÆTERNA SEPVLTIS.

OMNE DONVM PERFECTVM A DEO,IMPERE A DIABO.

AVREOLVS PHILIPPVS THEOPHRASTVS.

Paracelsus traveled and visited a number of universities, but he rejected medical training based on the ideas of Galen and Ibn Sina (see page 33). He is said to have made a bonfire of the works of Ibn Sina, to show he disagreed with them.

Paracelsus

The Swiss physician Theophrastus von Hohenheim, more commonly known as Paracelsus (1493–1541), challenged many of the beliefs about medical treatments held by most Renaissance doctors.

Paracelsus did not accept the theory of the four humors, believing instead in a theory known as the doctrine of signatures. This theory, based on folk medicine traditions, identified the properties of plants by their similarity to the part of the body being treated. For example, the walnut resembles a brain, so it was used to treat brain diseases. While incorrect, this was an important development in the history of medicine.

Physicians and Surgeons

From the 13th century onward, anyone wanting to become a fully qualified **physician** had to go to a university. This meant that women became automatically excluded from the profession, as they were not allowed to study at a university at that time. Medical training took many years, and many of the best—and wealthiest—English students chose to go abroad for part of their training, particularly to the famous medical schools at the universities of Padua and Bologna, in Italy, and Montpellier, in France.

This painting shows William Harvey (center) carrying out a **dissection** on the body of Thomas Parr. Parr was believed to have been 152 years old when he died.

Medical students studied the works of the ancient Greek writers Hippocrates and Galen, as well as famous physicians from the Islamic world such as Abdullah ibn Sina, also known an Avicenna (c. 980–1037). (You can find out more about Ibn Sina in the *Medieval Medicine* book in this series.) They read these texts in Latin or Greek, and lectures were delivered in Latin. They may also have observed some practical work, but most of their training was based on ideas. New ideas, such as the work of Vesalius (see pages 8–9) and Harvey (see pages 14–17), often took many years to be accepted. Many physicians continued to resist any questioning of the authority of Galen and the theory of the four **humors**.

THOMAS SYDENHAM
(1624–1689)

Thomas Sydenham trained as a physician at the University of Oxford, in England, but he believed that doctors learned far more by practical experience at a patient's bedside. He emphasized the importance of observing and describing symptoms in order to decide on the correct treatment. He introduced the use of laudanum (opium) and gave the first description of **scarlet fever**.

Did you know?
Sydenham became known as the "English Hippocrates" because of his careful observation of patients. This was a practice that had been encouraged by the famous ancient Greek scholar Hippocrates.

Training to be a surgeon

While physicians studied the theory of the human body, they did not undertake treatment that involved cutting the body. This was left to **barber-surgeons**, or surgeons. From the 14th century, surgeons were organized in guilds, which were trade organizations that set standards and protected their members. Surgeons did not attend a university. Instead, they learned their trade by being apprenticed to more experienced surgeons. This meant that surgery was still open to women. However, by the 18th century, surgery was being taught in European universities, effectively closing the profession to women.

Surgery

Surgeons were far less expensive to consult than physicians. They dealt with a range of complaints, including broken limbs, cuts and wounds, and skin conditions. They performed operations—for example, on swellings—as well as amputations. However, major surgery was usually a last resort in the Renaissance period.

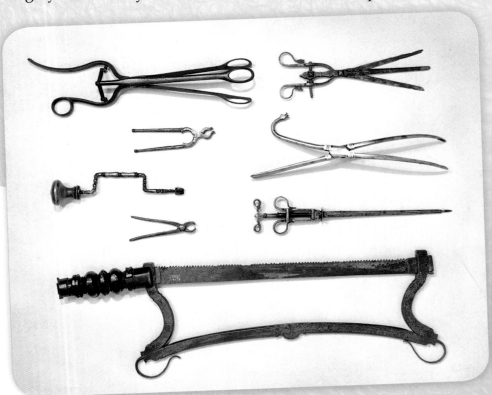

These are some examples of surgical instruments used in the 16th and 17th centuries.

▶

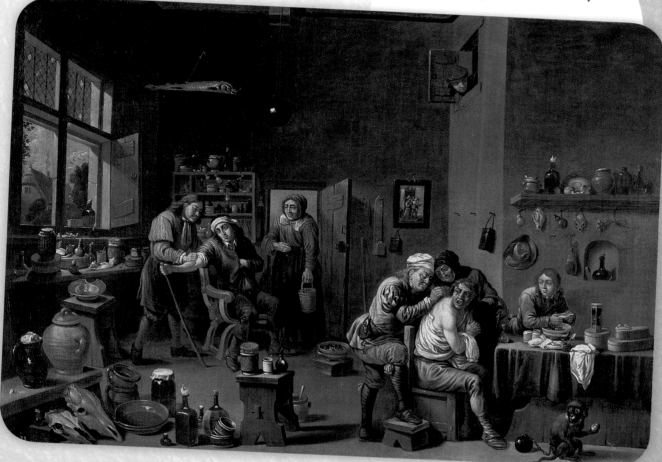

The three main challenges facing a surgeon were pain, infection, and bleeding. Surgeons needed to work quickly to try to avoid the death of a patient from shock and blood loss during an operation. To take the edge off the pain, some patients drank alcohol or herbal drinks, while others covered their noses with sponges soaked in opium. Surgeons' tools were not cleaned or **sterilized**, as they are today, so the risk of infection in the wound was very high.

For all these reasons, the types of surgery undertaken in the Renaissance were limited. One of the most complicated operations was lithotomy—the removal of "stones" from the bladder or kidneys that caused great pain and could result in death if not removed.

Caring for the Sick

When people became sick during the Renaissance period, the most likely place for them to receive treatment was at home, and the most likely people to care for them were the women of the household. Women nursed the sick, cleaned, and prepared food. Many also knew about growing medicinal herbs and preparing remedies.

In many communities, wealthier women were expected to play a part in caring for the sick of local families, and girls were taught the basics of medicine as part of their education. We know of the work of one of these women from the records she kept of her treatments. From her writing, it is clear that Grace Mildmay was able to widen her medical knowledge by reading the works of Galen, Ibn Sina, and Paracelsus (see page 31).

Wise women or witches?

Many people turned to healers such as wise women and traveling **quacks**. Wise women had knowledge of traditional medicine that had often been passed down through generations. They were, however, often under suspicion of using magic and witchcraft. The fear of witches increased during the 16th century, resulting in many witchcraft trials and executions.

This 16th-century print shows the burning of three women accused of being witches. So-called witches were often blamed for outbreaks of the **plague** and other unexplained events.

This painting shows a traveling quack selling potions to customers at a fair.

Quacks

Traveling quacks were healers who usually had little or no medical training. They sold herbal remedies for a wide range of common aches and pains as well as conditions such as blindness. They traveled from place to place, often putting on a show to attract business—and moving on quickly before their deception was discovered. Quacks continued to operate long into the 19th century.

However, not all quacks were deliberately trying to deceive their customers. Some would have believed in their products and believed that they were providing an important service. They sold remedies to people who had few other sources of medical care, and many people would have been satisfied that these treatments were helping their conditions.

GRACE MILDMAY
(1552–1620)

Mildmay was the daughter of a wealthy family in England. As a child, she was instructed in medicine and the basics of surgery by her governess. After her marriage to Anthony Mildmay in 1567, Mildmay made up large batches of medicines that were dispensed around the neighborhood. She kept records of the diseases she came across, as well as recipes for her remedies.

Did you know?
Mildmay dispensed medical help free of charge, and she became well known for her charity.

Midwives

Many women practiced as midwives. The quality of skill and knowledge varied, but most served an apprenticeship under an experienced midwife. In England, midwives were licensed by the Church. To obtain a license, they had to swear an oath to make their services available to both rich and poor, not to switch babies, not to engage in sorcery (magic), not to mutilate the baby, and to ensure the baby was baptized. They were also required to keep men out of the birthing chamber unless the services of a **physician** or surgeon were required. Despite the services of midwives, childbirth was a dangerous time for women. Complications during the birth killed many babies and sometimes the mother, too. There were also no **anesthetics** to ease the pain or **antiseptics** to deal with infection.

Jane Sharp, a midwife working in the 17th century, wrote the first English manual of midwifery. *The Midwives Book; or The Whole Art of Midwifery Discovered* (1671) gave practical advice to both parents and midwives. However, Sharp was particularly critical of a development in midwifery—the rise of man-midwives. This trend was set in motion by surgeons such as Ambroise Paré, who discovered a way to turn a baby in the womb in order to deliver it safely. Some surgeons began to add midwifery to their practice and to attend births, even when there was no medical emergency.

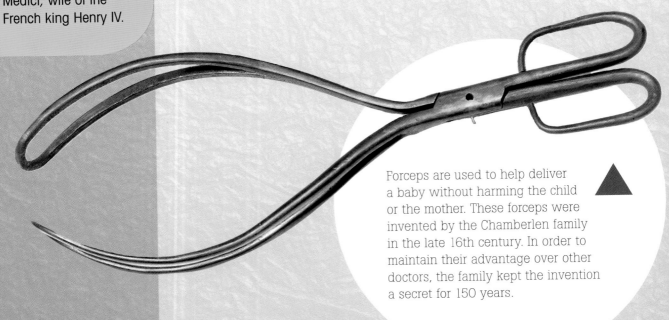

Forceps are used to help deliver a baby without harming the child or the mother. These forceps were invented by the Chamberlen family in the late 16th century. In order to maintain their advantage over other doctors, the family kept the invention a secret for 150 years.

Hospitals

In medieval Europe, the first hospitals were set up in monasteries and nunneries. They were places where the poor, elderly, and needy were cared for, rather than being centers of medical treatment. In fact, people with infectious diseases were not allowed to enter most hospitals. Hospitals later became places of charity, where sick poor people were cared for and given free medical treatment.

This woodcut shows a woman recovering from childbirth on a bed, while a midwife washes and tends to the baby.

ISLAMIC HOSPITALS

The first European hospitals were based on models from the Islamic world. Large hospitals, such as those in Baghdad, Cairo, and Damascus, were built from the ninth century CE onward. These hospitals combined medical treatment and education, with areas for treatment as well as lecture rooms and libraries for study. As the Islamic world became more fragmented in the 14th century, these hospitals fell into decline.

Model hospitals

Renaissance Italy had the most respected hospitals in Europe. When English King Henry VII decided to found a hospital in London, he turned to the Santa Maria Nuova Hospital in Florence, Italy, as his model. The Santa Maria Nuova was founded in 1288 with 12 beds. By the early 16th century, it had 100 beds in each of the men's and women's sections, as well as 50 more beds in smaller rooms.

Henry VII died before work on his new hospital began, so it was left to his son Henry VIII to build the Savoy. Whereas the Santa Maria Nuova in Florence treated only sick poor people, the Savoy gave priority to the sick, but it also took in cripples, the blind and infirm, and beggars. The sick were allowed to stay in the hospital until they were well, while the others were turned out every morning.

This 16th-century painting shows a hospital in Germany.

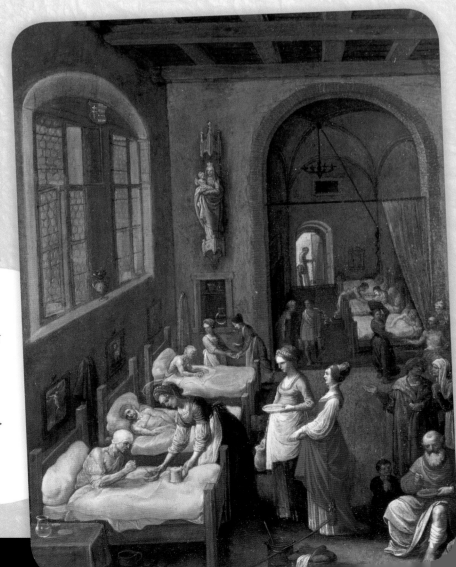

This is an engraving of a plague hospital in Vienna in 1679. It is estimated that around 76,000 people died in the city during this outbreak of the disease.

Regular outbreaks of plague led many city authorities to establish isolation hospitals, known as pesthouses, outside towns and cities. The pesthouse built to serve the Italian city of Milan was surrounded by a moat and had guard towers to prevent inmates from escaping. In 1630, many thousands of victims were sent to this pesthouse in an attempt to keep the **epidemic** under control.

Other isolation hospitals housed **syphilis** sufferers. In many Italian cities, victims of syphilis were refused entry to normal hospitals, so places of treatment for "incurables" were set up.

In conclusion

The Renaissance was a time of exploration and questioning in many fields, including that of medical knowledge. People began to challenge and reject some of the theories that had come down from the ancient Greeks and Romans and been accepted for centuries. A new foundation of knowledge, learned through experimentation and observation, set the scene for the revolution in science and medicine that followed.

Timeline

1430s	Johannes Gutenberg develops a method of printing involving movable type. Books could now be produced quickly, cheaply, and in large numbers. Mass printing was key to the rapid spread of knowledge and new ideas during the Renaissance period.
1490s	The first outbreaks of **syphilis** in Europe occur
1492	Christopher Columbus makes his first voyage to the Americas
c. 1503	Leonardo da Vinci makes detailed drawings of **anatomy**, based on **dissections**
1512	The Savoy Hospital opens in London, England
1518	The Royal College of **Physicians** is founded in London
1519	Hernan Cortés and his men arrive in Mexico
c. 1530s	Paracelsus pioneers mineral and chemical remedies
1540	The dissolution (closure) of monasteries by King Henry VIII ends. These closures had put a stop to hospital building in England.
1543	Andreas Vesalius publishes *De humani corporis fabrica* Nicolaus Copernicus publishes his theory that Earth orbits around the Sun
1545	Ambroise Paré publishes *Method of Treating Wounds*
1546	Girolamo Fracastoro develops the theory that disease is passed on by tiny particles or "seeds"
1571	Nicolas Monardes publishes *Joyfull Newes out of the Newe Founde Worlde*
1590s	The first workable compound microscope is developed

1597	John Gerard publishes *Great Herball*
1603	Hieronymus Fabricius describes the system of **valves** in **veins**
1628	William Harvey publishes *Concerning the Motion of the Heart and Blood*
c. 1630s	Cinchona bark (containing quinine) is first brought to Europe from Peru
1636	Pioneering French midwife Louise Bourgeois dies
1658	Samuel Pepys undergoes surgery to remove a bladder stone
1660	The Royal Society is founded in London
1661	Marcello Malpighi uses a microscope to observe and describe the **capillary** network
1664–1666	The Great **Plague** of London occurs
1665	Robert Hooke publishes *Micrographia*
1671	Jane Sharp publishes *The Midwives Book; or The Whole Art of Midwifery Discovered*
1672	Richard Wiseman publishes *Treatise on Wounds* and, four years later, in 1676, *Several Chirurgical [Surgical] Treatises*
1674	Anton van Leeuwenhoek uses a microscope to observe tiny living things such as protozoa and **bacteria**
1689	Thomas Sydenham, known as the "English Hippocrates," dies
1720	The last major outbreak of the plague occurs in Marseilles, France

Glossary

anatomy science of the structure of the human body

anesthetic substance used in operations to stop a patient from feeling pain

antiseptic prevents infection or contamination from germs and microbes (tiny living things)

apothecary person, mainly in the medieval and Renaissance periods, who prepared and dispensed medicines and remedies

artery blood vessel that carries blood away from the heart

astrological related to astrology, the study of the movements of planets and stars, which some people believe influence human affairs

bacteria (singular: bacterium) group of single-celled microbes (tiny living things) that inhabit almost all environments on Earth

barber-surgeon another name for a surgeon. In the medieval period, barber-surgeons shaved and cut hair to provide their daily income and also performed basic surgery.

bloodletting cutting veins to release blood

capillary one of the tiny blood vessels through which oxygen, nutrients, and wastes are exchanged between the blood and the tissues

cauterize in medieval and Renaissance medicine, to "seal" wounds by applying boiling oil or hot irons

curator keeper or manager, often in a museum

diagnose identify the nature of a disease or injury through examination

dissect cut something up to learn about and understand its inner structure

dissection process of cutting something up to learn about and understand its inner structure

dysentery disease transmitted through water or food that is contaminated by human excrement

epidemic rapid spread of a disease through an area or population

gout condition that causes inflamed and swollen joints

herbal book that describes herbs and their uses

humor in medieval medical theory, one of the four important fluids that control the body

latrine toilet

ligature cord used in surgery, especially to tie up a bleeding artery

optic nerve nerve that sends information from the eye to the brain

physician person qualified to practice medicine

plague bacterial disease that is easily passed on

quack unqualified person who claims to have medical knowledge

scarlet fever disease that causes a rash and bright red tongue. It was a major killer before it was treatable with antibiotics.

smallpox disease that causes a rash characterized by pus-filled blisters. It was a major killer and often left survivors terribly scarred and sometimes blind.

sterilize make free of bacteria

syphilis sexually transmitted disease

typhoid disease transmitted through water or food that is contaminated by human excrement

unsanitary dirty and unhygienic

valve device that regulates, directs, or controls the flow of a fluid

vein one of the blood vessels that carries blood back to the heart

Find Out More

Books

Dawson, Ian. *Renaissance Medicine* (The History of Medicine). New York: Enchanted Lion, 2005.

Fullick, Ann. *Medical Technology* (Sci-Hi Science and Technology). Chicago: Raintree, 2012.

Hartman, Eve, and Wendy Meshbesher. *The Scientists Behind Medical Advances* (Sci-Hi Scientists). Chicago: Raintree, 2011.

Mullins, Lisa. *Science in the Renaissance* (Renaissance World). New York: Crabtree, 2009.

Yount, Lisa. *William Harvey: Discoverer of How Blood Circulates* (Great Minds of Science). Berkeley Heights, N.J.: Enslow, 2008.

Web sites

www.knowitall.org/kidswork/hospital/history/renaissance/index. html
This history of medicine includes facts about the Renaissance.

www.nlm.nih.gov/exhibition/paracelsus/index.html
Find out more about Paracelsus and his work on this web site.

http://science.discovery.com/videos/100-greatest-discoveries-shorts-william-harvey-blood.html
Visit this web site to see a video explaining the importance of William Harvey's discoveries about how the blood circulates.

Places to visit

The Exploratorium, San Francisco, California
www.exploratorium.edu

The Health Museum, Houston, Texas
www.mhms.org

International Museum of Surgical Science, Chicago, Illinois
www.imss.org

Metropolitan Museum of Art, New York City
www.metmuseum.org

National Museum of Health and Medicine, Washington, D.C.
nmhm.washingtondc.museum

More topics to research

Learn more about discoveries, events, and other developments:

- the effect of the Gutenberg printing press on the spread of knowledge and new ideas

- the anatomical drawings of Leonardo da Vinci

- the long life of Thomas Parr (1483–1635)

- traveling quacks and the potions they sold

- midwives and male midwives

- the history of Renaissance hospitals

- the role of disease in the collapse of the Aztec and Inca empires

- The cover of this book shows a detail from a painting called *The Surgeon-Barber* by a follower of David Teniers the Younger. It shows a man being operated on by two surgeons. What does the painting tell you about medical practices in the Renaissance period? Can you think of any reasons why surgeries today look so different from those in the past?

Index